If Teapots Could Talk

Fun Ideas for Tea Parties

Gloria Hander Lyons

Blue Sage Press

If Teapots Could Talk: Fun Ideas for Tea Parties

Inquires should be addressed to:

Blue Sage Press
48 Borondo Pines
La Marque, TX 77568
www.BlueSagePress.com

ISBN-13: 978-0-9790618-2-0
ISBN-10: 0-9790618-2-2

Library of Congress Number: 2007901849

First Edition: March 2007

The information in this book is true and complete to the best of our knowledge. All recommendations are made without guarantee on the part of the author or Blue Sage Press. The author and publisher disclaim any liability in connection with the use of this information.

Printed in the United States of America

Table of Contents

Introduction
If Teapots Could Talk

An afternoon tea party is a great way to entertain your friends and family. Whether you're planning an elegant Victorian Christmas tea party or a wild and crazy "Mad-Hatter" tea party, your guests will enjoy the festivities.

Invented in the mid 1800's by the Duchess of Bedford in an attempt to stave off hunger pangs until the evening meal was served, afternoon tea quickly caught on in other English households, as well. The Duchess began a whole new trend that is still enjoyed today.

The very "civilized" practice of tea time forces us to slow our frantic, modern-day pace and take a brief time out to relax and enjoy the company of friends. Sharing delectable treats on our prettiest china shouldn't be considered a luxury that we rarely experience.

Using the tea time tips, recipes and party ideas included in this book, you can host a beautiful tea party to lavish on yourself and friends. So get out those teapots and create fond memories of lively conversation and laughter and fun, the way our ancestors have done for many years.

If only all those teapots could talk!

There are few hours in life more agreeable
than the hour dedicated to the ceremony known as
afternoon tea.

~Henry James, *The Portrait of a Lady*

All About Tea

Afternoon Tea Facts

Types of Tea

Preparing the Tea

Pouring the Tea

Afternoon Tea Party Facts

Afternoon tea is usually held between three and five o'clock in the afternoon. It is also called "low tea" because it's usually served in a sitting room where low tables (like a coffee table or tea cart) are placed near sofas or chairs.

Many Americans confuse the term "high tea" with an afternoon tea. High tea is actually a supper and refers to the height of the table (a dining table) where the food is served, with everyone seated around the table. High tea is served between five and six o'clock. Unlike the dainty treats served at an afternoon tea, this tea includes more hearty dishes, such as shepherd's pie.

An afternoon tea party is a festive affair, so plan to use your best dishes and teacups. Dainty tea sandwiches (both savory and sweet) and scrumptious cakes, cookies and pastries will delight the guests at your event.

Use pretty platters and tiered serving trays to present your tea time fare. And don't forget to include a sampling of scones, which are usually served with jam, honey and Devonshire or clotted cream.

On the following pages, learn how to make all the delectable treats you'll need for a proper afternoon tea, including the perfect pot of tea.

Types of Tea

All tea comes from the dried leaves of the Camellia sinensis plant. The leaves contain tannin (an astringent), caffeine (a stimulant) and an essential oil that gives it its own distinct flavor.

This flavor is also affected by the altitude where the tea is grown; the soil type and amount of rainfall and sunlight it receives; when the tea is picked; and how it is processed.

Tea falls into three basic categories, depending on how the leaves are processed:

- Black teas are the most popular in America. The leaves are crushed and then fermented before drying. They have a stronger flavor than the other teas.

- Oolong teas are only partially fermented and then steamed. Their leaves are a greenish-brown color, and the flavor is milder than black tea.

- Green teas are not fermented, just steamed, which preserves their green color and delicate flavor.

There are thousands of varieties of teas—which come mostly from Sri Lanka, India, Indonesia, Kenya and other East African countries. The tea you buy at tea shops or grocery stores can be a blend of 20 to 30 varieties, which are carefully selected by expert tea tasters to produce a particular quality and flavor that is unique to each brand.

A few of the more commonly known blends are: English Breakfast, a blend of strong teas from India and Ceylon; Jasmine, either green or a mix of black and green teas mixed with jasmine flowers; and Lapsang Souchong, from China, which has a smoky aroma and rich flavor.

Two of the most rare and expensive teas are: white tea, made in China from the buds of tea leaves, has a very mild and naturally sweet flavor; and Darjeeling, grown in the mountains of Nepal and known as the "Champagne of Teas", has a golden color and muscatel aroma.

Scented teas are flavored with essential oils of flowers, fruits and spices. One example is Earl Grey, an afternoon tea favorite, which contains bergamot (orange) oil.

Storing Tea:

Always buy tea in small quantities and store it in an airtight container in a cool, dark, dry place, because it tends to absorb moisture and odors. Also, the unique essential oils that give the tea its flavor can evaporate more quickly when exposed to air.

Teatime Tidbit: Orange Pekoe is not a flavor of tea. The term "pekoe", which means "little", is simply a grade of tea leaf size that means "small".

Preparing the Tea

To make a perfect pot of tea:

- Start with fresh, cold tap water in the tea kettle and bring it to a boil
- Use a glass or china teapot (never metal) for brewing your tea
- Fill the teapot with boiling water to warm it
- Pour out the water and place about 1 teaspoon of loose tea for each cup of water needed into the teapot
- For most types of tea, such as black, pour boiling water over the tea and steep for 3 to 5 minutes, depending on the type of tea and the strength desired
- For brewing green and white teas, use a slightly cooler water temperature

Tea that is brewed too long will have a bitter taste. Stir the water for more even brewing and then pour into cups through a strainer.

Tea Balls:

Using a tea ball to hold the loose tea during the steeping process is easier than straining the tea into cups through a strainer. It does, however, take longer to brew the tea than using loose tea leaves. Using a tea ball will also allow you to remove the tea leaves from the teapot so the tea doesn't brew too long. Just remember to fill the ball only about half full, because the tea leaves will expand when they are wet.

How to Remove Caffeine from Tea

If you're concerned about the affects of caffeine, but can't find your favorite flavor of tea in a decaffeinated version, follow the steps listed below to remove most of the caffeine from any tea:

- Pour boiling water over the tea leaves
- Allow the leaves to steep for 30 seconds
- Pour out the water, saving the leaves
- Pour boiling water over the same leaves and steep for the desired amount of time

Teatime Health Tip: Drinking tea is a great way to get the recommended daily fluids your body needs. Tea also contains antioxidants, which are thought to be beneficial for the heart.

Tea Bags

Tea bags are another convenient way to make tea. They were invented in 1904 by a New York tea merchant who sent samples to customers in tiny, hand-sewn silk bags instead of tea tins. The bags were so popular he received hundreds of orders for them.

The tea particles in tea bags are much smaller than loose tea and therefore brew more quickly. If you allow the bag to steep too long, the tea will be bitter.

Don't squeeze the tea bag when removing it from the tea because it can release bitter oils into your tea. Never use a tea bag twice. The particles are too small to retain enough flavor to produce a second cup of tea.

If you can't find your favorite flavor of tea in the form of a convenient tea bag, make your own. You can purchase disposable paper tea bags or self-sealing tea bags on-line very inexpensively. (See ordering information in the index.)

Teatime Tip: To flavor your teabags, store them in an airtight jar with citrus peel, vanilla beans or cinnamon sticks.

Pouring the Tea

In most cases, the hostess pours the tea at her afternoon tea party, but occasionally, she might bestow the honor on a friend. Unlike serving coffee, tea is never poured several cups at a time because it cools very quickly. The person pouring the tea prepares each cup individually, according to a guest's personal preference.

When pouring the tea, first ask each guest if she prefers strong or weak tea. You should always keep a separate teapot filled with hot water to dilute strong tea.

Next, ask how many lumps of sugar she prefers, then whether she wants milk or lemon (never both). The lemons should be cut into thin slices – not wedges.

After preparing the guest's tea, hand the teacup and saucer to the guest and begin to prepare the next guest's tea.

The guests can help themselves to the tea party food, which is displayed on pretty serving platters. Be sure to provide appropriate serving pieces such as tongs or pie servers.

Teatime Etiquette: When attending a tea party, it's fun to dress up and wear gloves, but always remove your gloves as you enter the room. It isn't considered proper to shake hands, eat food or drink tea while wearing gloves.

Tea Recipes

Flavored Teas

Herbal Teas

Tea Blends

Flavored Teas

There are many flavored teas available in the form of loose tea leaves or tea bags at tea shops or your local grocery store that you can use for brewing the tea at your tea party. But it's also fun to experiment with different combinations of flavors to create a special brew for your event.

The recipes listed below will give you a few ideas.

Chocolate Tea

2 tablespoons black tea leaves
1 tablespoon cocoa powder
1 teaspoon dried grated orange peel
1/4 cup brown sugar, firmly packed

Add all the ingredients to a warmed teapot, along with 6 cups of boiling water. Stir and then steep for 5 minutes. Stir again and strain into cups.

Serve with milk, and provide additional brown sugar for your guests if needed.

Apple Tea

Black tea leaves
Clear apple juice
Sugar to taste
Cinnamon sticks

This tea is brewed using apple juice instead of water. Place 1 teaspoon of tea per cup of juice needed into a warmed teapot. Heat required amount of apple juice in a saucepan until boiling. Pour juice into teapot and steep for 5 minutes. Stir and then strain tea into cups. Serve with a cinnamon stick. Sweeten with sugar if needed.

Apricot Orange Tea

2 1/2 cups apricot nectar
1-1/2 cups orange juice
2 cups water
1 cinnamon stick, broken
8 whole cloves
2 tablespoons black tea leaves

Combine apricot nectar, orange juice, water, cinnamon and cloves in a medium-size saucepan. Heat mixture just until boiling. Add tea leaves to warmed teapot. Pour boiling juice mixture into teapot and steep for 5 minutes. Stir and strain into cups. Sweeten with sugar.

Teatime tip: Flavor sugar cubes for tea by storing them in a jar with whole cloves, vanilla beans or cinnamon sticks. You can also decorate the sugar cubes for a tea party with icing flowers to make them more festive.

Cranberry Tea

3 cups water
3 cups cranberry juice cocktail
1 cinnamon stick, broken
8 whole cloves
2 tablespoons black tea

Combine water, cranberry juice, cinnamon stick and cloves in a medium sauce pan. Heat mixture just until boiling. Add tea leaves to warmed teapot. Pour boiling juice mixture into teapot and steep for 5 minutes. Stir and strain into cups. Sweeten with sugar.

Mulled Tea

5 cups of water
3/4 cup orange juice
1/4 cup lemon juice
8 whole cloves
3 cinnamon sticks, broken
2 tablespoons black tea leaves

Combine water, orange juice and lemon juice in a medium sauce pan; heat mixture just until boiling.

Add cloves, cinnamon sticks and tea leaves to warmed teapot. Pour boiling juice mixture into teapot and steep for 5 minutes. Stir and strain into cups. Sweeten with sugar.

Herbal Teas

Herbal teas do not contain tea leaves, and therefore have no caffeine. They are made from a combination of herbs, spices, citrus zest and flowers.

There are hundreds of possibilities for herbal teas and tea blends, and they're easy and inexpensive to make at home. You can create a tea blend from your favorite herb flavors or one blended specifically to make you feel energized or relaxed, or even to lift your spirits.

- Herbs for creating a relaxing tea are: lavender, sage, chamomile and rose

- For an energizing tea, use rosemary, peppermint and lemon

- For an uplifting brew, use bergamot, geranium, orange and rosemary

Many flavors of herbal teas are available at your local supermarket or tea shop in the form of tea bags, which are very convenient for enjoying this refreshing, caffeine-free beverage.

Teatime Tip: Chamomile tea is the perfect choice for bed time. It has a gentle flavor and contains a natural sedative to help you fall asleep.

Herbs have been used for thousands of years for brewing tea. In America, after the Boston Tea Party, when the colonists dumped all the black tea they owned into the harbor, they were forced to use herbal teas instead, calling them "liberty teas". They brewed herbal teas from rosemary, lavender, thyme, sage, mint and lemon balm.

How to Make Herbal Tea:

To make an herbal tea, also known by the French term *tisane,* use one tablespoon of fresh herbs or one teaspoon of dried herbs for each cup of boiling water. Rinse the teapot with boiling water to warm it, drain the water and then add the herbs. Pour boiling water over the herbs and allow them to steep for 5 to 7 minutes.

Since herbal teas don't turn darker as they steep, as regular teas do, you need to judge the strength by taste rather than sight. Strain the tea into cups and serve.

If you don't have a local source for buying dried herbs, you can always order them on-line and have them shipped to your door. See the index for ordering information.

Note: Always make sure the herbs you use to make herbal teas are pesticide free and intended for culinary use.

Try the following herbal tea recipes or make up your own blend from your favorite herbs.

Calming Tea Blend

1 tablespoon dried rosemary leaves
1 tablespoon dried spearmint leaves
1 tablespoon dried culinary lavender buds
2 teaspoons dried culinary chamomile flowers
1/2 teaspoon whole cloves

Adjust herb measurements to suit your own taste or omit any herbs you don't like. Blend the herbs together and store in an airtight container away from heat and light.

To prepare: Place 1 to 1-1/2 teaspoons of tea mixture per cup of water needed into a warmed teapot.

Pour boiling water over the herbs and steep for about 5 minutes. Stir and strain into cups. Serve with honey or sugar and lemon.

Note: Lavender should be avoided by women who are pregnant or nursing. Also, it should not be used with preparations containing iron and/or iodine.

Herbal Tea Blend

2 tablespoons loose tea leaves
2 teaspoons dried sage leaves
1 teaspoon dried thyme leaves
1/2 teaspoon dried lemon peel

Combine all ingredients and store in an airtight container away from heat and light.

To prepare: Place 1 to 1-1/2 teaspoons of tea blend in a warmed teapot for each cup of water needed.

Pour boiling water over tea and steep 3 to 5 minutes. Stir and strain into cups.

Sweeten with honey or sugar and serve with lemon slices.

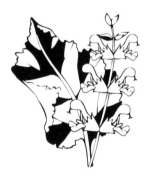

Lavender and Lace Tea

1/2 teaspoon dried culinary lavender buds*
1 teaspoon dried culinary rose petals*
2 tablespoons black tea leaves

Mix all ingredients and store in an airtight container. This recipe will make one six-cup pot of tea. Place tea mixture into warmed teapot. Add six cups of boiling water and steep for 3 to 5 minutes. Strain into tea cups.

*Culinary lavender and rose petals are pesticide-free. See ordering information in the index

> **Note:** Lavender should be avoided by women who are pregnant or nursing. Also, it should not be used with preparations containing iron and/or iodine.

Teatime Tip: Try adding some of the following to your herbal tea: honey or brown sugar; lemon, lime or orange juice; spices, such as ginger, cinnamon, or vanilla; or a teaspoon of your favorite fruit jelly.

Herb Sugar

Flavored sugars can add a special touch to any tea party. Add 1 or 2 teaspoons of dried herbs—such as lemon balm, mint or lavender—to a cup of granulated sugar. If desired, add a drop or two of a food coloring (green for mint, purple for lavender, yellow for lemon, etc.).

Blend on high in a blender or food processor until herbs and sugar are thoroughly mixed. Dry on a cookie sheet for several hours, if you've added food coloring, before storing in an airtight container.

Tea Party Menu

Scones
Flavored Butters &
Spreads
Tea Sandwiches
Savory Appetizers
Tea Time Sweets

Preparing the Tea Party Menu

The possibilities for tasty treats to serve the lucky guests at your tea party are unlimited. Choose a variety of foods, both savory and sweet, such as dainty tea sandwiches, pastries, cakes and muffins. And don't forget the scones.

Your food choices should not only taste delicious, but look pretty as well.

The traditional menu for afternoon tea served in the late 1800's was tea, bread, butter and cakes, but the tea menu today usually includes three courses:

- Savories: Tiny sandwiches or appetizers
- Scones: Served with jam and Devonshire cream
- Pastries: Tarts, cookies, cakes and other sweets

Having a theme for your tea party (such as Valentine's Day, garden party, or "Lavender and Lace") is not only fun, it can also help you choose the food for your party.

The following recipes might give you a few ideas to include on the menu.

Scones

You can't have a proper afternoon tea party without serving scones. There are thousands of recipes for these taste-tempting treats—either savory or sweet.

Scones are similar to baking powder biscuits, either cut into traditional, triangle-shaped wedges or in rounds, using a biscuit cutter. Serve your scones warm with Devonshire or clotted cream and jam or flavored butters.

Tips for making tender scones:

- For these scone recipes, you don't need to sift the flour, but do stir the flour first, then lightly spoon it into the measuring cup and level off with a knife.
- Mix the dry and liquid ingredients in separate bowls before combining.
- Don't over mix when blending the dry and liquid ingredients or your scones will be tough.
- Don't twist the biscuit cutter when stamping out scones. This causes uneven baking and the scones may turn out lopsided.
- Don't over bake your scones or they will be dry. Oven temperatures can vary, so check them about five minutes before baking time is up.

Cream Scones

2 cups flour
1/4 cup sugar
1-1/2 teaspoons baking powder
1/2 teaspoon baking soda
1/4 teaspoon salt
6 tablespoons unsalted butter
1 large egg, slightly beaten
1/2 cup half-and-half
1 teaspoon vanilla extract

Preheat oven to 400°. In a large bowl, combine flour, sugar, baking powder, baking soda and salt. Cut in butter with a pastry blender until mixture resembles coarse crumbs.

Mix together egg, half-and-half and vanilla extract; stir into dry ingredients just until moistened. Add a bit more flour if dough seems too sticky. Turn dough out onto a lightly floured surface; knead 8-10 times or until smooth.

Pat into a 7" circle, about 3/4" thick. Cut into 8 pie-shaped wedges. Or roll dough to 3/4" thickness and cut out circles with a 2-1/2" biscuit cutter, or 1-1/2" cutter for mini scones. Brush tops with milk and sprinkle with sugar.

Place 1" apart on lightly greased cookie sheet. Bake for 18-20 minutes (15-18 minutes for mini scones) or until golden brown. Serve warm with jam and clotted cream or flavored butter.

For variations: Add 1 teaspoon dried, grated orange or lemon peel, 2/3 cup semi-sweet chocolate chips, 2/3 cup chopped nuts, or 1/2 cup of dried fruit, such as cranberries or raisins.

Apple Scones

2 cups flour
1/3 cup sugar
1-1/2 teaspoons baking powder
1/2 teaspoon baking soda
1/2 teaspoon ground cinnamon
1/4 teaspoon salt
6 tablespoons unsalted butter
1 large egg, slightly beaten
1/3 cup half-and-half
1 teaspoon vanilla extract
2/3 cup apples, peeled and finely chopped

Preheat oven to 400°. In a large bowl, combine flour, sugar, baking powder, baking soda, cinnamon and salt. Cut in butter with a pastry blender until mixture resembles coarse crumbs. Mix together egg, half-and-half and vanilla extract; stir into dry ingredients just until moistened. Stir in apples. Turn dough out onto a lightly floured surface; knead 8-10 times or until smooth.

Pat into a 7" circle, about 3/4" thick. Cut into 8 pie-shaped wedges. Or roll dough to 3/4" thickness and cut out circles with a 2-1/2" biscuit cutter, or 1-1/2" cutter for mini scones. Brush tops with milk and sprinkle with sugar or cinnamon sugar. Place 1" apart on lightly greased cookie sheet. Bake for 18-20 minutes (15-18 minutes for mini scones) or until golden brown.

Serve warm with Brown Sugar Cinnamon Butter, page 32.

Teatime Etiquette: The proper way to eat a scone: Open the scone horizontally in half with a knife. Spread just enough jam and Devonshire cream on the scone for one bite. Then repeat until the scone is gone!

Chocolate Chunk Scones

2 cups flour
1/3 cup sugar
1-1/2 teaspoons baking powder
1/2 teaspoon baking soda
1/4 teaspoon salt
6 tablespoons unsalted butter
1 large egg, slightly beaten
1/2 cup half-and-half
1 teaspoon vanilla extract
3 squares of semi-sweet baking chocolate, chopped

Preheat oven to 400°. In a large bowl, combine flour, sugar, baking powder, baking soda and salt. Cut in butter with a pastry blender until mixture resembles coarse crumbs.

Mix together egg, half-and-half and vanilla extract; stir into dry ingredients just until moistened. Stir in chocolate. Add a bit more flour if dough seems too sticky. Turn dough out onto a lightly floured surface; knead 8-10 times or until smooth.

Pat into a 7" circle, about 3/4" thick. Cut into 8 pie-shaped wedges. Or roll dough to 3/4" thickness and cut out circles with a 2-1/2" biscuit cutter or a 1-1/2" cutter for mini-scones. Brush tops with milk and sprinkle with sugar.

Place 1" apart on lightly greased cookie sheet. Bake for 18 to 20 minutes (15-18 minutes for mini scones) or until golden brown.

Serve warm with Chocolate Butter, page 33 or Devonshire Cream, page 35.

Cherry Cream Scones

1/2 cup dried cherries, chopped
2 cups flour
1/3 cup sugar
1-1/2 teaspoons baking powder
1/2 teaspoon baking soda
1/4 teaspoon salt
6 tablespoons unsalted butter
1 large egg, slightly beaten
1/3 cup half-and-half
1 teaspoon vanilla or almond extract

Soak cherries in 3/4 cup boiling water for 10 minutes. Drain well and set aside. Preheat oven to 400°.

In a large bowl, combine flour, sugar, baking powder, baking soda and salt. Cut in butter with a pastry blender until mixture resembles coarse crumbs.

In a separate bowl, mix together egg, half-and-half and extract; stir into dry ingredients just until moistened. Stir in cherries. Turn dough out onto a lightly floured surface; knead 8-10 times or until smooth.

Roll or pat dough to 3/4" thickness and cut out circles or shapes with a 1-1/2" to 2" cookie cutter. Brush tops with milk and sprinkle with sugar. Place 1" apart on lightly greased cookie sheet. Bake for 15 to 18 minutes, or until golden brown.

Serve warm with Cherry Butter, page 34.

Christmas Scones

1/4 teaspoon ground cinnamon
1 tablespoon sugar
2 cups all-purpose flour
1/3 cup sugar
1-1/2 teaspoons baking powder
1/2 teaspoon baking soda
1/4 teaspoon salt
6 tablespoons butter
1 large egg, slightly beaten
1/3 cup sour cream
2 tablespoons orange juice
1 teaspoon dried, grated orange peel
1/2 cup dried cranberries, chopped

Preheat oven to 400°. In a small cup, mix cinnamon and 1 tablespoon sugar; set aside.

In a large bowl, combine flour, sugar, baking powder, baking soda and salt. Cut in butter with a pastry blender until mixture resembles coarse crumbs. In a separate bowl, mix together egg, sour cream, orange juice and orange peel; stir into dry ingredients just until moistened. Stir in cranberries. Turn dough out onto a lightly floured surface; knead 8-10 times or until smooth.

Roll or pat dough to 3/4" thickness and cut out with a 2-1/2" star-shaped cookie cutter. Brush tops with milk and sprinkle with cinnamon sugar. Place 1" apart on lightly greased cookie sheet. Bake for 15 to 18 minutes, or until golden brown. Makes 8 - 10 scones.

Serve warm with Brown Sugar Cinnamon Butter, page 32.

Cheddar and Garlic Scones

2 cups flour
1-1/2 teaspoons baking powder
1/2 teaspoon baking soda
1/2 teaspoon salt
1/4 teaspoon garlic powder
1/8 teaspoon cayenne pepper
    (optional)
6 tablespoons butter
2/3 cup shredded cheddar cheese
1 large egg, slightly beaten
1/2 cup half-and-half

Preheat oven to 400°. In a large bowl, combine flour, baking powder, baking soda, salt, garlic powder and pepper. Using a pastry blender, cut in butter until mixture resembles coarse crumbs. Stir in cheese.

In a separate bowl, combine egg and half-and-half. Stir egg mixture into dry ingredients, just until moistened. Add a bit more flour if dough seems too sticky. Turn dough out onto a lightly floured surface; knead 8-10 times or until smooth.

Pat into a 7" circle, about 3/4" thick. Cut into 8 pie-shaped wedges. Or roll dough to 3/4" thickness and cut out circles with a 2-1/2" biscuit cutter or a 1-1/2" biscuit cutter for mini scones. Place 1" apart on a lightly greased cookie sheet. Bake for 18 to 20 minutes (15-18 minutes for mini scones), or until golden brown. Serve warm with butter.

Tea Time Tip: If you're serving several varieties of scones at your tea party, make mini-scones instead of regular size scones. Pat dough into a 3/4" thickness and cut out using a 1-1/2" to 2" round cutter. Reduce baking time to 15 – 18 minutes or until golden brown.

Savory Sausage Scones

8 ounces mild or hot bulk pork sausage
1/4 cup finely chopped onion
2 cups all purpose flour
1-1/2 teaspoons baking powder
1/2 teaspoon baking soda
1/2 teaspoon dried oregano, crushed
1/2 teaspoon salt
6 tablespoons butter
1 large egg, slightly beaten
1/2 cup half-and-half

Cook sausage and onion until browned, breaking up sausage as it cooks. Drain off excess fat; cool slightly.

Preheat oven to 400°. In a large bowl, combine flour, baking powder, baking soda, oregano and salt. Using a pastry blender, cut in butter until mixture resembles coarse crumbs. Stir in sausage and onion.

In a separate bowl, combine egg and half-and-half. Stir egg mixture into dry ingredients, just until moistened. Add a bit more flour if dough seems too sticky. Turn dough out onto a lightly floured surface; knead 8-10 times or until smooth.

Pat into a 7" circle, about 3/4" thick. Cut into 8 pie-shaped wedges. Or roll dough to 3/4" thickness and cut out circles with a 2-1/2" biscuit cutter or a 1-1/2" biscuit cutter for mini scones. Place 1" apart on a lightly greased cookie sheet. Bake for 18 to 20 minutes (15-18 minutes for mini scones) or until golden brown. Serve warm with butter.

Rosemary Scones

2 cups all-purpose flour
1 tablespoon sugar
1-1/2 teaspoons baking powder
1/2 teaspoon baking soda
1/2 teaspoon salt
1 tablespoon fresh rosemary, chopped or 1 teaspoon
     dried rosemary, crushed
1/4 cup butter or margarine (4 tablespoons)
1/2 cup sour cream
1 egg, slightly beaten

Preheat oven to 400°. In a large bowl, combine flour, sugar, baking powder, baking soda and salt. Cut in butter with a pastry blender until mixture resembles coarse crumbs. In a separate bowl, mix together egg, sour cream and rosemary; stir into dry ingredients just until moistened.

Turn dough out onto a lightly floured surface; knead 8-10 times or until smooth. Roll or pat dough to 3/4" thickness and cut out with a 2-1/2" biscuit cutter or a 1-1/2" biscuit cutter for mini scones. Place 1" apart on lightly greased cookie sheet. Optional: Brush tops with melted butter. Bake for 18 to 20 minutes (15-18 minutes for mini scones) or until golden brown. Serve warm with Herb Butter, page 34.

Scone Tea Sandwiches

Bake savory mini scones, like Rosemary or Cheddar and Garlic. Split in half horizontally. Spread a thin layer of softened butter (mixed with a bit of prepared mustard if you like) over the cut sides. Fill with a layer of thinly sliced smoked or baked ham.

Flavored Butters and Spreads

Honey Butter

1/2 cup unsalted butter, softened
2 tablespoons honey

In a small bowl, beat ingredients together until fluffy. Refrigerate until ready to serve. Soften for 15-20 minutes before serving.

Brown Sugar & Cinnamon Butter

1/2 cup unsalted butter, softened
2 tablespoons brown sugar, firmly packed
1/2 teaspoon ground cinnamon

In a small bowl, beat all ingredients together until fluffy. Refrigerate until ready to serve. Soften for 15-20 minutes before serving.

Chocolate Butter

1/2 cup unsalted butter, softened
2 tablespoons confectioner's sugar
2 tablespoons cocoa powder

In a small bowl, beat ingredients together until fluffy. Refrigerate until ready to serve. Soften for 15-20 minutes before serving.

Strawberry Butter

1/2 cup unsalted butter, softened
2 tablespoons strawberry preserves
2 tablespoons confectioner's sugar

In a small bowl, beat ingredients together until fluffy. Refrigerate until ready to serve. Soften for 15-20 minutes before serving.

Herb Butter

1/2 cup butter, softened
2 tablespoons fresh herbs chopped, or 2 teaspoons of dried herbs, (use any combination of the following: parsley, basil, tarragon, thyme, chives, sage or rosemary)

In a small bowl, beat ingredients together. Refrigerate until ready to serve. Soften for 15-20 minutes before serving.

Cherry Butter

1/2 cup unsalted butter, softened
2 tablespoons cherry preserves
2 tablespoons confectioner's sugar

In a small bowl, beat ingredients together until fluffy. Refrigerate until ready to serve. Soften for 15-20 minutes before serving.

Clotted Cream

Also called "Devonshire cream", clotted cream is made in England by scalding the cream from unpasteurized milk until it thickens. Real clotted cream is sold in some specialty stores the United States and on-line, but you can make a good substitute using the following two recipes.

"Clotted" Cream

1 cup whipping cream
2 tablespoons confectioner's sugar
1/2 cup sour cream

Beat whipping cream and sugar until soft peaks form. Gently fold in sour cream. Chill until ready to serve. Mixture will keep up to 4 hours in the refrigerator.

"Devonshire" Cream

1 (8-oz.) package cream cheese, softened
1/4 cup sour cream
1/4 cup whipping cream
3 tablespoons granulated sugar
1 teaspoon vanilla

Beat cream cheese until fluffy, then beat in remaining ingredients until well blended. Cover and refrigerate until ready to serve.

Lemon Curd

Lemon curd is a thick, tangy sauce that is spread on scones and pound cake. It can also be used as a filling for tarts. Many gourmet food stores, as well as some large supermarkets, sell lemon curd in jars, or you can try your hand at making your own using the following recipe.

Lemon Curd

1/3 cup fresh lemon juice, strained
1 cup granulated sugar
3 large eggs
1/4 cup unsalted butter
1 tablespoon finely grated lemon zest

Combine juice, sugar and eggs in the top of a double boiler. Whisk together until well blended. Place pan over simmering water and cook, stirring constantly, until thickened and smooth, about 18 - 20 minutes. Do not allow mixture to boil.

Remove the top of the double boiler from hot water and stir in the butter, a little at a time, until blended. Stir in lemon zest. Mixture will continue to thicken as it cools. Makes about 1-3/4 cups of lemon curd.

Store in a covered container in the refrigerator until ready to serve. It will keep for up to one week in the refrigerator. Spread on slices of pound cake or scones, or use to fill tartlet shells for Lemon Curd Tartlets (see page 53).

Note: For a less tangy version, whip 1/2 cup of heavy cream to soft peaks and fold into lemon curd.

Tea Sandwiches

Dainty tea sandwiches served on pretty platters are a must for an afternoon tea party. Whether you're serving warm, open faced sandwiches or cold fillings sandwiched in between slices of bread, the possibilities are endless.

When making tea sandwiches, use thinly sliced, dense breads such as white, whole wheat, rye and pumpernickel. Always spread the bread lightly with softened butter before adding the filling. This keeps the filling from making the bread soggy.

Assemble the sandwiches on full slices of bread and refrigerate them, then, just before serving, trim off crusts and cut each one into pieces, either four triangles or four squares.

You can also cut the bread into pretty shapes using cookie cutters to make them even more appealing. Prepare five to six sandwiches per guest.

The following is a list of recipes that you might want to serve at your tea party, but any favorite filling such as chicken salad, egg salad or flavored cream cheese would also be good.

Tomato and Cucumber Sandwiches

1 (8 ounce) package cream cheese, softened
1 cucumber, peeled and thinly sliced
3 medium tomatoes, thinly sliced
Salt and pepper to taste
16 slices of whole wheat or pumpernickel bread
Butter or margarine, softened

Lightly butter each slice of bread. Spread about 2 tablespoons of cream cheese on 8 of the slices.

Arrange a layer of cucumber slices and then tomato slices on top of the cream cheese. Sprinkle with salt and pepper and top with the remaining buttered bread slices.

Trim away crusts and cut into 4 triangles or squares. Refrigerate until ready to serve. Makes 32.

Chive Cream Cheese Cucumber Tea Sandwiches

1 (8-ounce package) cream cheese, softened
2 teaspoons dried chives
1 cucumber, peeled and thinly sliced
Salt and pepper to taste
16 slices of whole wheat or white bread
Butter or margarine, softened

Lightly butter each slice of bread. In a small bowl, blend cream cheese and chives. Spread 2 tablespoons of cream cheese mixture on 8 of the slices.

Arrange a layer of cucumber slices on top of the cream cheese. Sprinkle with salt and pepper and top with the remaining buttered bread slices. Trim away crusts and cut into 4 triangles. Refrigerate until ready to serve. Makes 32.

Strawberry Cream Cheese Tea Sandwiches

1/2 cup (4 ounces) cream cheese, softened
1/4 cup strawberry jam (or any flavor you like)
12 slices white bread
Butter or margarine, softened

Lightly butter each slice of bread. In a small bowl, blend cream cheese and jam. Spread 2 tablespoons of cream cheese mixture on 6 of the slices.

Trim away crusts and cut into 4 triangles or use small, about 1-1/2", cookie cutters or biscuit cutter to cut out shapes (circles, diamonds, hearts, etc.) Refrigerate until ready to serve. Makes about 24.

Ham & Melon Tea Sandwiches

1/3 pound thinly sliced smoked ham
1/4 cantaloupe, peeled, seeded and thinly sliced
8 slices of whole wheat or pumpernickel bread
Butter or margarine, softened

Lightly butter each slice of bread. Place a layer of ham on 4 of the bread slices. Top with a layer of melon and remaining slices of buttered bread. Trim crusts and cut into 4 triangles or squares. Refrigerate until ready to serve. Makes 16.

Roast Beef & Cream Cheese Tea Sandwiches

1/4 cup cream cheese, softened
2 tablespoons mayonnaise
1 teaspoon chives
1/8 teaspoon garlic powder
1/2 pound thinly sliced, cooked roast beef from the deli
24 small, pimiento-stuffed olives and toothpicks
12 slices of whole wheat or white bread
Butter or margarine, softened

Lightly butter each slice of bread. In a small bowl, blend cream cheese, mayonnaise, chives and garlic powder. Spread about 1 tablespoon of cream cheese mixture on 6 of the slices.

Arrange a layer of roast beef on top of the cream cheese. Top with the remaining buttered bread slices. Trim away crusts and cut into four triangles or squares. Place an olive on a toothpick and insert into top of each sandwich. Refrigerate until ready to serve. Makes 24.

Smoked Turkey and Cranberry Sandwiches

1/4 cup whole cranberry sauce
1 teaspoon Dijon mustard (or to taste)
1/3 pound thinly sliced, smoked turkey
8 slices whole wheat bread
Butter or margarine, softened

In a small bowl, mix cranberry sauce and mustard.

Lightly butter each slice of bread with softened butter.

Spread about 1 tablespoon of cranberry sauce mixture on 4 slices of bread and top with slices of turkey. Cover with remaining slices of bread.

Trim crusts and cut into 4 triangles or squares. Refrigerate until ready to serve. Makes 16.

Salmon and Dill Sandwiches

1 cup canned salmon, drained and bones removed
1/4 cup mayonnaise
1 tablespoon finely chopped green onion
1 teaspoon dried dill weed (or to taste)
12 slices of thinly sliced whole wheat bread
Butter or margarine, softened

In a small bowl, mix together salmon, dill, green onion and mayonnaise. Lightly butter each slice of bread with softened butter. Spread about 3 tablespoons of salmon mixture on 6 of the bread slices and top with the remaining bread slices. Trim crusts and cut into 4 triangles or squares. Refrigerate until ready to serve. Makes 24.

Guacamole Chicken Sandwiches

1/2 cup guacamole
1 large, cooked chicken breast, thinly sliced
8 slices of whole wheat, rye or pumpernickel bread
Mayonnaise
Butter or margarine, softened

Lightly butter all the slices of bread with the softened butter. Spread about 2 tablespoons of guacamole on 4 of the buttered slices of bread. Place chicken slices on guacamole. Spread the remaining 4 slices of bread with mayonnaise and place on top of chicken. Trim crusts and cut into 4 triangles or squares. Makes 16.

Ham and Pineapple Pinwheels

1/2 cup cream cheese, softened
1/4 cup ground, smoked ham
1/4 cup crushed pineapple, well drained
8 slices of soft, white or whole wheat bread

In a small mixing bowl, blend together the cream cheese, ham and pineapple. Trim crusts off bread and flatten bread slices slightly with a rolling pin or fingers.

Spread 2 tablespoons of filling onto each slice of bread. Roll up jelly-roll fashion and wrap in plastic wrap. Chill at least 2 hours or until firm enough to slice. Remove plastic wrap and slice each roll into 5 pieces (3/4" slices). Recipe makes 40 pinwheels.

Olive Pecan Pinwheels

1/2 cup cream cheese, softened
2 tablespoons pimento stuffed olives, finely chopped
2 tablespoons toasted pecans*, finely chopped
6 slices of soft, white or whole wheat bread

In a small bowl, blend the cream cheese, olives and pecans. Trim crusts off bread and flatten with rolling pin or fingers. Spread 2 tablespoons of filling onto each slice of bread. Roll up jelly-roll fashion and wrap in plastic wrap. Chill at least 2 hours or until firm enough to slice. Remove plastic wrap and slice each roll into 5 pieces (3/4" slices). Makes 30 pinwheels.

*Toast pecans in a dry skillet over medium heat, stirring frequently until golden brown.

Mint Egg Salad
Tea Sandwiches

4 large hard-boiled eggs
3 tablespoons mayonnaise
1 tablespoon fresh mint leaves, finely chopped
      (or 1/2 to 1 teaspoon dried mint, crushed)
1/2 teaspoon prepared yellow mustard
Salt and pepper to taste
Butter or margarine, softened
10 slices of white bread

Peel eggs and place in a medium bowl. Mash the eggs with a fork. Add mayonnaise, salt, pepper and mint; stir until well blended. Cover and refrigerate for at least one hour to blend flavors.

Lightly butter each slice of bread. Spread 5 of the slices with about 3 tablespoons of the egg mixture. Top with remaining slices of bread. Trim away the crusts and cut each sandwich into 4 triangles or squares. Makes 20.

Dill Egg Salad Tea Sandwiches

Substitute 1/2 tablespoon of fresh dill or 1/2 teaspoon dried dill weed for the mint leaves in the Mint Egg Salad recipe. Prepare as directed for Mint Egg Salad. Optional: add 2 teaspoons of dill pickle relish to the Dill Egg Salad.

Savory Appetizers

Mini Zucchini and Cheese Quiches

2 large eggs
1/2 cup half-and-half
1/4 teaspoon onion powder
1/4 teaspoon salt
Dash of pepper
1/2 cup shredded Swiss cheese
1/2 cup shredded zucchini
1 (15 ounce) package of refrigerated pastry
       (2 crusts for 9" pie)

Preheat oven to 350°. Unroll pastry and cut into 24 circles using a 3" biscuit cutter. Line mini muffin cups with dough. Place about 1 teaspoon of zucchini in each muffin cup. In a measuring cup with a pouring spout, beat eggs, half-and-half, onion powder, salt and pepper. Fill muffin cups 3/4 full with egg mixture. Sprinkle about one teaspoon of cheese on top of each quiche. Bake 20-25 minutes until pastry is golden brown and centers are set. Let stand 10 minutes before removing from pan. Cool on wire rack. Serve warm or cold.

Mini Bacon Quiches

2 large eggs
1/2 cup half-and-half
1/4 teaspoon onion powder
1/4 teaspoon salt
Dash of pepper
6 slices bacon, crisply fried and crumbled
1/2 cup shredded Swiss cheese
1 (15 ounce) package of refrigerated pastry
        (2 crusts for 9" pie)

Preheat oven to 350°. Unroll pastry and cut into 24 circles using a 3" biscuit cutter. Line mini muffin cups with dough. Divide bacon evenly among the muffin cups.

In a measuring cup with a pouring spout, beat eggs, half-and-half, onion powder, salt and pepper. Fill muffin cups 3/4 full with egg mixture. Sprinkle about one teaspoon of cheese on top of each quiche.

Bake 20-25 minutes until pastry is golden brown and centers are set. Let stand 10 minutes before removing from pan. Cool on wire rack. Serve warm or cold.

Chicken Salad Puffs

1 package (17.3 oz.) frozen puff pastry, thawed
2 cups chopped cooked chicken
2/3 cup finely chopped celery
2 tablespoons finely chopped green onion
2/3 cup mayonnaise
1/4 cup chopped, toasted almonds*
Salt and pepper to taste

In a medium bowl, combine chicken, celery, green onion, mayonnaise, almonds, salt and pepper. Mix until well blended. Chill for several hours to blend flavors.

To prepare puffs, preheat oven to 400°. Unroll pastry dough onto lightly floured surface. Cut puff pastry into assorted shapes (hearts, diamonds, circles) using 2-1/2" cookie or biscuit cutters. Place 1" apart on ungreased baking sheet. Bake for 12 - 15 minutes or until puffed and golden. Cool on wire racks.

Cut puffs in half, horizontally. Spoon about 2 teaspoons of chicken mixture into puffs and replace tops. Makes about 32 puffs.

* Toast almonds in a dry skillet over medium heat, stirring frequently until golden brown. Cool before adding to chicken salad mixture.

Stuffed Cherry Tomatoes

24 cherry tomatoes
6 ounces cream cheese, softened
1/2 teaspoon dried, crushed basil leaves
Dash of salt

Cut tops from tomatoes and scoop out insides. Drain upside down on paper towels. In a small bowl, beat cheese, basil and salt together.

Fill each tomato with cream cheese mixture. Refrigerate until ready to serve.

Olive Cheese Puffs

1 cup shredded Cheddar cheese
1 cup all-purpose flour
1/2 cup butter (1 stick), softened
24 pimiento-stuffed olives, well-drained

Preheat oven to 400°. In a medium bowl, mix cheese, flour and butter until well blended. Pinch off about one rounded teaspoon of dough and flatten in the palm of your hand. Wrap dough around one stuffed olive, sealing all edges.

Arrange the wrapped olives on a lightly greased cookie sheet. Bake for 15-18 minutes until lightly browned. Remove puffs to a wire rack to cool.

Fruit and Cheese Mini Turnovers

1/2 cup butter or margarine (1 stick), softened
1 cup all-purpose flour
1/2 cup grated Cheddar cheese
1/4 cup fruit preserves (strawberry, apricot or orange marmalade)

Preheat oven to 375°. In a medium bowl, combine butter, flour and cheese. Add a bit of milk if dough seems too dry. Turn dough out onto a lightly floured surface; knead 8-10 times or until smooth. Roll out to about 1/8" thickness and cut out circles using a 3" biscuit cutter.

Place about 1/2 teaspoon of fruit preserves in center of each circle. Fold dough in half and seal edges by pressing with the tines of a fork. Place turnovers on a lightly greased baking sheet.

Bake 12-15 minutes or until light brown. Remove from baking sheet and cool on a wire rack. Makes about 12.

Cucumbers with Shrimp Salad

1-1/4 cups cooked shrimp, finely chopped
2/3 cup finely chopped celery
1 tablespoon minced green onion
1/3 cup mayonnaise
Salt and pepper to taste
1 cucumber

Combine shrimp, celery and onion in a medium bowl.

Add mayonnaise, salt and pepper. Lightly mix until well blended. Cover and chill for 2 hours to blend flavors.

Slice cucumber into 1/8" slices. Top each slice with shrimp salad. Refrigerate until ready to serve. Makes about 20.

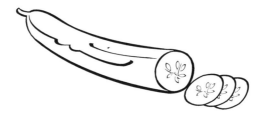

Tea Time Sweets

Any favorite recipe for cakes or cookies can be served at an afternoon tea, but bite-sized treats such as miniature cheesecakes, tiny tarts, muffins or petit fours are especially appealing when served on pretty tiered platters or serving trays. The recipes below will offer a wide variety of delectable treats for your next tea party.

Chocolate Dipped Strawberries

8 ounces semi-sweet chocolate chips
24 large, ripe strawberries

Place chocolate chips into a microwave-safe measuring cup. Microwave on high for 30 seconds then stir. Repeat until chocolate is melted and smooth. Do not allow to boil.

Make sure the strawberries are completely dry before dipping. If you use refrigerated strawberries, allow them to come to room temperature. Dip them into the melted chocolate. Set on waxed paper to cool. Refrigerate until ready to serve. Serve at room temperature.

Pecan Tartlets

Tartlet Crust:

1/2 cup butter, softened
4 ounces cream cheese, softened
1 cup flour
1/4 cup confectioner's sugar
1/2 teaspoon vanilla extract

Blend all ingredients to form dough. Press one tablespoon of dough into 20 ungreased mini-muffin pan cups to form tartlet shells.

Filling:

1/2 cup finely chopped pecans
1 egg
3/4 cup brown sugar
2 tablespoons butter, melted
1/8 teaspoon salt
1/2 teaspoon vanilla extract

Preheat oven to 350°. Sprinkle one teaspoon of pecans into bottom of each shell.

In a measuring cup with a pouring spout, combine egg, sugar, butter, salt and vanilla extract. Fill each shell with filling. Bake for 20-25 minutes or until crusts are light brown. Let stand in pan 5 minutes then remove to wire rack to cool.

Lemon Curd Tartlets

Tartlet Crust:

1/2 cup butter, softened
4 ounces cream cheese, softened
1 cup flour
1/4 cup confectioner's sugar
1/2 teaspoon vanilla extract

Preheat oven to 350°. Blend all ingredients to form dough. Press one tablespoon of dough into 20 ungreased mini-muffin pan cups to form tartlet shells. Bake for 10 minutes or until light brown. Let stand in pans 5 minutes then remove to wire rack to cool.

Lemon Curd:

Prepare the Lemon Curd recipe on page 36.

Fill cooled tartlet shells with lemon curd. Refrigerate until ready to serve.

If desired, top with sweetened whipped cream or non-dairy whipped topping before serving.

Mini Cheesecakes

Crust:
1 cup graham cracker crumbs
3 tablespoons sugar
3 tablespoons butter or margarine, melted

Filling:
2 (8-ounce) packages cream cheese, softened
3/4 cup sugar
2 eggs
1 teaspoon vanilla extract

Preheat oven to 350°. Line 18 muffin cups with paper liners. Mix crust ingredients together and press about 1 tablespoon of mixture into bottom of each cup. Beat cream cheese until fluffy. Add sugar, eggs and vanilla extract, blending well.

Spoon cream cheese mixture into cups; fill about 2/3 full. Bake for 15 - 20 minutes or until set. Cool before removing from pans. Chill. Top with pie filling (cherry or blueberry) before serving, if desired.

Chocolate Mini Cheesecakes

Crust: Substitute chocolate graham cracker crumbs in the crust recipe above.

For Filling: Place 1/2 cup semi-sweet chocolate chips into a microwave-safe bowl. Microwave on high for 30 seconds then stir. Repeat until chocolate is melted and smooth. Cool slightly and stir into cream cheese mixture before adding eggs. Bake as directed for Mini Cheesecakes.

Zucchini Bread Tea Sandwiches

To make bread:
1 cup grated zucchini (about 1 large)
1 cup granulated sugar
1/2 cup vegetable oil
1 teaspoon vanilla extract
2 eggs
1-1/2 cups flour
1 teaspoon cinnamon
1/2 teaspoon salt
1/2 teaspoon baking powder
1/2 teaspoon baking soda
1/2 cup chopped pecans

Preheat oven to 350°. In a large mixing bowl, combine zucchini, sugar, oil, vanilla extract and eggs. Beat until well blended. In a separate bowl, mix flour, cinnamon, salt, baking powder and baking soda. Stir into the zucchini mixture. Fold in pecans. Pour into a 9 x 5 x 3" greased and floured loaf pan. Bake 55-60 minutes or until done. Remove from pan and cool on wire rack.

To make sandwiches:
Slice the zucchini bread into very thin slices.

Sandwich Filling:
1 cup cream cheese, softened
1 cup well-drained, crushed pineapple

Blend cream cheese and pineapple. Spread about 1 or 2 tablespoons of filling on one slice of zucchini bread. Top with another slice of bread. Cut each sandwich into four rectangles.

Mint Nut Tea Bread

1-1/4 cups all-purpose flour
1/2 cup brown sugar, firmly packed
1-1/2 teaspoons baking powder
1/4 teaspoon baking soda
1/4 teaspoon salt
1/4 teaspoon ground cinnamon
1/2 cup chopped walnuts
1/2 cup applesauce
2 tablespoons vegetable oil
1 egg, slightly beaten
1 teaspoon dried mint or 1 tablespoon fresh mint, chopped

Preheat oven to 350°. Lightly grease and flour a small loaf pan (8" X 4"). In a large bowl, mix flour, sugar, baking powder, baking soda, salt, cinnamon and nuts. In a separate bowl, blend together applesauce, oil, mint and egg. Add to flour mixture, stirring until well blended.

Pour into prepared loaf pan and bake for 30-35 minutes or until done. Turn out onto wire rack to cool. To serve, slice into 1/2" slices. Cut each slice into four rectangles.

Pumpkin Tea Bread

1-3/4 cups all-purpose flour
1-1/2 cups granulated sugar
1 teaspoon baking soda
1/2 teaspoon cinnamon
1/4 teaspoon salt
2 eggs, slightly beaten
1/2 cup vegetable oil
1 cup canned pumpkin purée
1/2 cup chopped pecans

Preheat oven to 350°. Lightly grease and flour a 9" X 5" loaf pan. In a large bowl, combine flour, sugar, baking soda, cinnamon and salt.

In a separate bowl, combine eggs, oil and pumpkin. Add to flour mixture and stir until well blended. Stir in nuts.

Pour into prepared loaf pan and bake 55-60 minutes or until done. Turn out onto rack to cool.

To serve, cut loaf into 1/2" slices and cut each slice into four rectangles.

Chocolate Chip Meringue Cookies

2 egg whites
1/2 cup sugar
1/2 teaspoon vanilla extract
1/8 teaspoon salt
1 cup (6 ounces) semi-sweet chocolate chips
1/2 cup finely chopped pecans

Preheat oven to 325°. Beat egg whites and vanilla extract until soft peaks form. Gradually beat in sugar and salt until mixture is very stiff and glossy. Fold in chocolate chips and pecans.

Drop by teaspoonfuls onto a cookie sheet lined with foil. Bake for 30 minutes or until golden. Cookies should be completely dry inside. Cool completely before removing from cookie sheet. Makes about 36.

Peaches and Cream Mini Muffins

1/2 cup sugar
1 egg
1/4 cup vegetable oil
1/4 teaspoon vanilla extract
1/2 cup sour cream
1 cup all-purpose flour
1/4 teaspoon baking soda
1/4 teaspoon salt

1/2 cup finely diced peaches (canned or fresh)

Preheat oven to 375°. Grease mini-muffin pans. In a large bowl, beat egg with sugar, oil and vanilla extract. Stir in sour cream.

In a separate bowl, mix together flour, salt and baking soda. Stir dry ingredients into egg mixture until well blended. Add peaches. Fill muffin cups 3/4 full. Bake for 15-18 minutes until golden brown. Makes 24.

Easy Petit Fours

Cake:

1 (9" X 5") store-bought pound cake loaf, either fresh or frozen and thawed (or make your own from a mix)

Icing:

2/3 cup hot water
2/3 cup light corn syrup
1/2 teaspoon vanilla extract
7 cups confectioner's sugar
Food coloring in desired choice of colors

In a large bowl, stir the corn syrup into the hot water. Add the vanilla extract. Using a whisk, blend in the confectioner's sugar until smooth. Divide into two or more smaller bowls and tint each one a different color.

Slice pound cake into 3/4" slices. Cut each slice into 4 rectangles about 1-1/2" X 2" or cut out desired shapes from the slices using a small (about 1-1/2") cookie cutters.

Arrange cake pieces on a wire rack and place the rack on a cookie sheet to catch the drippings. Pour icing over tops and sides of petit fours. After icing is set, coat petit fours with another layer of icing if desired. Let the icing dry completely before storing in a single layer in an airtight container. Makes about 32.

Tea Party
Ideas

Decorations

Party Themes

Tea Party Club

Tea Party Decorations

Whether you're having your tea party in a beautiful garden, a cozy kitchen, an elegant parlor or a pretty porch, you'll want to create a festive atmosphere with party decorations and table settings to match your party theme and colors.

Your tea table will be the focal point of the party, so get out your best tablecloths, napkins, teapots and china. The party theme will help you decide on the colors and choice of invitations, decorations, food and party favors.

Create an interesting centerpiece that fits your theme, such as pretty hats for a Victorian tea, a pot of herbs for a garden tea or wrapped packages for a Christmas tea.

Display the food on elegant trays or unique serving pieces that are raised at different heights to create interest in the display. You can use pans or bowls turned up-side down or sturdy boxes as risers to vary the heights of the serving platters. Cover the risers with a tablecloth or fabric.

Keep your party theme in mind when choosing serving dishes. For example, use hat boxes for a "Mad-Hatter" tea party, terracotta pots for a garden tea party or old-fashioned tins for a kitchen shower tea party.

Ask your guests to dress according to the party theme or color. They become part of the decorations, adding to the overall festive atmosphere of the tea party, and everyone feels like they are making a contribution.

Don't forget that the party fun begins with your invitation. A unique invitation will pique your guests' curiosity and create anticipation for your event. Get creative when choosing or making your invitations. They don't have to be printed on flat pieces of paper; they can be attached to a straw hat, printed on a package of garden seeds or tucked inside a heart shaped box.

A few ideas for tea parties are listed below, including fun ideas for invitations, decorations, menu choices, party games and activities and guest favors.

Use these suggestions to spark your creativity when planning your next tea party.

Teatime tip: For large parties, prepare a strong tea concentrate by pouring 4 cups of boiling water over 2/3 cup of tea leaves. Let stand 5 minutes, then stir and strain into a teapot. When ready to serve, pour about 2 tablespoons of concentrate into each cup, then fill cup with steaming hot water.

Bridal Shower
Tea Party

Host a bridal shower tea party where "tea parties" is your theme. The guests bring gifts that the bride will be able to use when she hosts her own tea parties.

A few gift suggestions are: teapots and elegant cup and saucer sets (either new or vintage), tiered serving platters, sugar tongs, tea strainers, tea caddies, tea balls, unusual flavors of tea, pretty napkins and a copy of this book.

- Your invitation can be a cut-out in the shape of a teapot. Enclose a pretty, blank recipe card asking each guest to write her favorite teatime treat or appetizer recipe on the card and bring it to the party. Collect the cards and bundle them in a satin ribbon to present to the bride.

- Cover your tea table with a white tablecloth and drape a garland of white tulle and silk greenery around the edges. Your centerpiece can be the wrapped gifts for the bride.

- For the menu, serve tea sandwiches, sugar cookies and petit fours (page 60) cut into the shape of teapots. Other choices might be Chocolate Chip Meringue Cookies (page 58) and Mini Cheese Cakes (page 54).

- For a fun activity, play the "What Did You See?" game. Prepare a tray on which you have arranged 10 or 12 tea-related items. Cover the items with a fabric napkin. When you are ready to play the game, give each guest a pen and piece of writing paper. Uncover the items on the tray and let your guests look at them for about 20 - 30 seconds. Recover the tray and ask your guests to write down as many of the items as they can remember. The guest who writes down the most correct items wins a prize. You can also place one item that is completely unrelated to the others on the tray to throw your guests off track. If you like, let the winner choose one item from the tray for her prize and present the remaining items to the bride as a gift.

  For a different version of this game, have an assistant who is not a guest at the party walk through carrying your tray so the guests can view the items. When the assistant leaves the room, ask your guests to write down as many details as they can remember about the assistant: what she was wearing, her hair color or eye color, etc. The guest with the most correct details wins a prize.

- For guest favors, collect tea cups and saucers from flea markets or garage sales. Place a few tea bags inside each one. Wrap each cup in a square of tulle, bringing the corners together and tie them with a pretty ribbon.

Tea-Tasting Party

Invite your friends to a tea-tasting event. You'll need to bone up on your tea facts, so you can show your guests how to compare the teas by noting their unique colors and scents.

- Attach your invitation to a real teabag of an unusual flavor of tea. Ask each guest to bring her favorite flavor of tea in the form of tea bags (or small plastic bags or sealable tea bags filled with one or two teaspoons of loose tea) for a tea bag exchange. Tell them how many to bring—one per guest attending.

- For your tea table centerpiece, create an arrangement of small baskets, lined with pretty fabric napkins to hold the teabags that each guest brings. Raise the baskets on small covered boxes of various heights for a more interesting display.

- Brew 3 or 4 flavors of tea for your event. You can find a wide variety of flavors in the form of teabags at tea shops. Or, if you really want to explore the world of tea, purchase a few unusual brands of loose tea or tea bags on-line. See the index for ordering information.

- Show off your teapot collection by using a different teapot for each flavor of tea, and label them so your guests will know each flavor.

- Since your guests will be drinking several cups of tea in order to taste them all, use demitasse cups, or pour just half a cup of tea into regular tea cups.

- Prepare a wide variety of teatime sweets and savory appetizers for your guests to enjoy. A few possibilities are: Cheddar and Garlic Scones (page 29), Chicken Salad Puffs (page 47), Zucchini Tea Bread Tea Sandwiches (page 55) and Pecan Tartlets (page 52).

- Ask each guest to talk about the special tea she brought to share: where it is from, how it tastes and why it is one of her favorites.

- For a fun activity, give each guest a pen and piece of writing paper and ask them to write down their answer to the following question: If you were a type of tea, what would you be and why? If your guests aren't familiar with different types of tea, have a chart on display with examples of tea and descriptions of each one. A few suggestions: English Breakfast, a blend that comes on strong; Jasmine, a mild mix with a sweet floral flavor; Lapsang Souchong, a smoky aroma and rich flavor; Earl Grey, a popular favorite, but a bit on the fruity side; a rare and expensive white tea with a naturally sweet flavor; and high-priced Darjeeling, known as the "Champagne of Teas". Place all the slips into a bowl. Draw out each slip and read the answer. See if the other guests can guess who wrote it.

- For favors, give each guest a pretty drawstring bag in which to place one tea bag of each flavor of tea that your guests brought to the party.

"Mad Hatter" Tea Party

Everyone likes to play "dress-up". Invite your friends to a tea party where each guest wears an outrageous or funny hat that she bought or made herself. You can find unusual ones at used clothing stores or garage sales.

- For the invitation, decorate tiny straw hats with ribbon and silk flowers. Write the party information on a pretty note card. Attach to the hat with ribbon. Place the invitation inside a small hatbox or gift bag lined with colorful tissue. Don't forget to tell your guests to wear their wild and crazy hats. Mail in a box or hand-deliver the invitations.

- Create an arrangement of pretty, decorated hats for your tea table centerpiece. You can go really wild with your party color choices for tablecloth, napkins and china for this event—the brighter the better.

- Use decorated hatboxes to serve some of your teatime treats, such as scones or tea sandwiches. Menu choices might include Mini Zucchini and Cheese Quiches (page 45), Roast Beef & Cream Cheese Tea Sandwiches (page 40) and Cucumbers with Shrimp Salad (page 50). For sweets try mini Apple Scones (page 25) with Brown Sugar & Cinnamon Butter (page 32) and Mini Cheesecakes topped with cherry pie filling (page 54).

- Have a fashion show where each guest models her hat on a runway. Award each guest a "prize" for her hat (funniest, most colorful, largest, smallest, most creative, etc.). Take lots of pictures of your guests wearing their fabulous hats or videotape the event and show it during the last half-hour of the party.

- Make special "hat" cookies for favors by using a cookie cutter to cut out 3" and 1-1/2" circles from sugar cookie dough, rolled out to about 1/4" thick. Bake the cookies as directed for your recipe (you can use prepared cookie dough if you like). Glue one 1-1/2" cookie to the center of one 3" cookie using icing. Decorate the cookies with colorful icing "ribbons" and "flowers". Place each cookie in a tiny hat box and tie with satin ribbon.

Valentine's Day Tea Party

Host a "fun and crafty" Valentine's Day tea party.

- The invitations should be in the shape of a heart or delivered in a small heart-shaped box. You can also use a vintage-style Valentine. Ask your guests to wear red or pink to your party.

- As much of the food as possible should be pink or red and/or in the shape of hearts. Serve cranberry tea (page 14), heart-shaped tea sandwiches, like Salmon & Dill (page 42) or Chicken Salad Puffs (page 47), Chocolate Dipped Strawberries (page 51) and heart-shaped Cherry Cream Scones tinted with red food coloring (page 27) and Cherry Butter (page 34).

- Your centerpiece can be a teapot filled with red roses (real or silk). Use a red tablecloth with a white lace overlay.

- For a fun activity, provide craft supplies (lace, beads, stickers, markers, colored paper, etc.) so each guest can make a pretty Valentine for her sweetheart. Give prizes for the best hand-made Valentine in several categories (most colorful, most creative, most sentimental, etc.).

- For favors, give foil-wrapped chocolates bundled with squares of red tulle and satin ribbon.

Lavender and Lace
Tea Party

Host an elegant lavender and lace tea party
to surprise and delight your guests.

- Print the invitation on lavender paper and trim with
  pretty lace. Ask your guests to wear lavender.

- Cover your table with a lavender table cloth with a
  white lace overlay. Your centerpiece can be a
  bouquet of lavender in a pretty teapot.

- Serve Lavender and Lace Tea (page 19). As much
  of the food as possible should be lavender-colored
  or purple, such as flavored cream cheese tea
  sandwiches (page 39), blueberry muffins or scones,
  mini-cheesecakes topped with a blueberry glaze
  (page 54) or try some of the lavender recipes listed
  below.

- For a fun activity, have all the guests sit in a circle.
  Give one guest a wrapped gift. Read the poem on
  page 75 and have the guests pass the gift to the
  person on their left each time they hear the word
  "lavender". The guest holding the gift at the end of
  the poem is the winner. You can also use two gifts,
  starting them at opposite sides of the circle. For a
  real challenge, have the guests pass the gifts in
  opposite directions around the circle.

- Party favors can be organza drawstring bags filled with culinary lavender and a recipe card attached on which you have written one of the lavender recipes you served at your tea party.

Note: Lavender should be avoided by women who are pregnant or nursing. Also, it should not be used with preparations containing iron and/or iodine.

Lavender has a strong flavor, very similar to rosemary, so limit the number of lavender offerings at your tea party to two or three out of six to eight choices of food for your guests.

The lavender used in cooking must be intended for CULINARY use (pesticide free). Use a clean coffee grinder or food processor to grind the dried lavender before measuring for the recipes.

You can find sources for ordering culinary lavender on-line by typing "lavender" into your search engine. Then have it shipped right to your door. See the ordering information after the index page for sources.

Lavender Egg Salad Tea Sandwiches

Follow the recipe for Mint Egg Salad Tea Sandwiches on page 44, except omit the mint and add 1/2 teaspoon of dried, ground lavender buds to the recipe. Mix and prepare sandwiches as directed in the recipe.

Lavender Tea Cookies

1/2 cup sugar
1/4 cup butter or margarine
1 egg
2 teaspoons dried, ground culinary
        lavender
1/4 teaspoon dried lemon peel
1 cup flour
1 teaspoon baking powder
1/8 teaspoon salt

Grind lavender in a coffee grinder or food processor before measuring. Preheat oven to 375°.

Cream together butter and sugar. Add egg, lavender and lemon peel; mix well.

In a separate bowl, blend the flour, baking powder and salt. Add the dry ingredients to the creamed mixture and mix well.

Drop by teaspoonfuls onto lightly greased cookie sheet. Bake about 12 - 14 minutes. Don't over-brown. Remove from oven and cool on wire racks. Makes about 18 cookies.

Lavender Scones

Add 2 teaspoons of ground, dried lavender to the Cream Scone recipe on page 24. You can also add a few drops of purple food coloring when blending the wet ingredients, if you like. Serve with Lavender Honey or Lavender Infused "Clotted Cream".

Lavender Honey

1 teaspoon dried lavender buds
1 cup honey

Wrap lavender in a cheesecloth bundle. Place honey and lavender in a microwave safe measuring cup and heat until very warm to infuse the lavender flavor. Let steep at least 30 minutes then discard lavender.

Lavender Infused "Clotted Cream"

Combine 1 cup heavy cream with 1 tablespoon dried lavender buds in small bowl. Cover and refrigerate for 8 hours to allow cream to absorb the lavender flavor. Strain cream and discard lavender. Use the cream in the "Clotted Cream" recipe on page 35. Add a few drops of purple food coloring to the cream if desired.

Lavender Poem Game

For a fun activity, have all your guests sit in a circle. Give one guest a wrapped gift. Read the poem below and have the guests pass the gift to the person on their left each time they hear the word "lavender". The guest holding the gift at the end of the poem is the winner. You can also use two gifts, starting them at opposite sides of the circle. For a real challenge, have the guests pass the gifts in opposite directions around the circle.

Lavender

You are cordially invited
to a lovely lavender tea.
So don a lavender outfit
and join me and my friends at three.

There'll be lots of lavender treats,
and lavender in the teapot.
Do you like lavender cheesecake,
Or lavender scones, I forgot?

We'll drink lavender tea with honey
and eat lavender cookies and cake.
And other lavender goodies,
I'll put in bags for you to take.

How about a lavender game?
Let's have lots more lavender fun!
We'll find out who the winner is
when this lavender poem is done!

Mommy & Me Tea

Don't forget the little ones when planning tea parties. Sharing tea with children can be a memorable event. This party is planned for children ages 6-10. Limit the guest list to about 8-10 people (4 mommies and 4 to 6 children).

- Your invitation can be a teapot cutout that your child decorates with markers or tea-related stickers. You can enlarge the one on page 77 using a copy machine and print it out on colored card stock, then cut it out. Write the party details on the back. Ask the guests to dress for a "traditional" tea: pretty dresses, white gloves and hats if they like.

- The centerpiece for your tea table can be children's toys, such as teddy bears and dolls holding child-size teapots and tea cups. Prepare a separate child-size tea table with 4-6 chairs for the children to sit while preparing food and eating.

- The activity at this party will be teaching the children tea-time etiquette and how to prepare treats for a tea party. Read "Pouring the Tea", page 10, and show them how to pour and prepare tea for each other, using small teapots, about 3-cup size. You can use decaffeinated tea if you prefer.

- Let them prepare tea sandwiches with flavored cream cheese (page 39) and use a 1-1/2" cookie cutter to cut out the shapes of their choice.

- Serve mini cream scones, page 24, (cut out with a 1-1/2" – 2" biscuit cutter) with jam and Devonshire cream, page 35. Show the children the proper way to eat a scone, page 25.

- Other menu choices might include Olive Pecan Pinwheels, page 43, Zucchini and Cheese Quiches, page 45, Ham & Melon Tea Sandwiches, page 40, Mini Cheesecakes, page 54, and Pumpkin Tea Bread, page 57.

- For favors, give each child a demitasse cup and saucer, wrapped in tulle and tied with a satin ribbon.

Enlarge and cut out the above design for your invitation.

Country Christmas Tea Party

Tea parties are a great way to celebrate holidays throughout the year. Plan a cozy Country Christmas tea party to welcome the Christmas holiday season.

- Tuck your invitation inside a small, patchwork Christmas stocking and mail it in a padded envelope. Ask your guests to wear the traditional Christmas colors of red and green.

- Cover your table with a homespun red or green plaid tablecloth or a patchwork quilt with a Christmas theme or colors. Your centerpiece can be a basket of evergreen boughs and pine cones.

- As much of the food as possible should be red or green and cut into the shapes of Christmas trees or stars.

- Serve Mulled Tea (page 14), Smoked Turkey and Cranberry Tea Sandwiches (page 41), Stuffed Cherry Tomatoes (page 48), Zucchini Bread (page 55) and Christmas Scones (page 28).

- For a fun activity, ask your guests to bring a wrapped "white elephant" gift (the most bizarre or useless item they can find—preferably old). Place all the gifts on a display table. Have each guest draw a number from one to the number of guests attending the party. The person who draws number one chooses a gift to unwrap. The person holding number two can either choose a new gift from the table or take the gift that has been unwrapped. Continue until all the gifts are opened.

- Guest favors can be bags of Mulled Tea Mix. Follow the recipe on page 14 and place whole cloves, cinnamon sticks and tea leaves in a small, plastic zipper-type bag. Place the bag in the center of an 8" square of homespun fabric. Bring the corners of the fabric together and tie with jute or ribbon. Attach a tag with the instructions for adding juice and water and steeping in a teapot.

Chocolate Tea Party

It's easy to plan a theme for a tea party based on a food flavor, and who doesn't love chocolate? Have a deliciously decadent Chocolate Tea Party for all things chocolate!

- Your invitation can be attached to a small bag of individually wrapped chocolates and mailed in a silver foil-covered box. Make sure the weather isn't too warm—you don't want your guests' treats to melt. Or, cut your invitation from chocolate colored card stock and write the party information using a silver paint pen. Glue on a border of silver-colored glitter for pizzazz.

- Cover your serving table with a chocolate-colored tablecloth or fabric and serve all your chocolate offerings on silver trays and tiered serving dishes. If you really want to get fancy, use a silver tea set for serving your chocolate tea.

- For true chocolate decadence, have a small chocolate fountain as your centerpiece. Cut up pieces of pound cake and fruit served on toothpicks to plunge into the flowing chocolate.

- There won't be any savory treats at this tea—it's all about sweets. Serve Chocolate Tea (page 12), Chocolate Chunk Mini Scones (page 26) cut out using a 1-1/2" biscuit cutter, along with Chocolate Butter (page 33), Chocolate Cheesecakes (page 54), and Chocolate-Dipped Strawberries (page 51).

- For a fun activity, give your guests a pen and writing paper. Ask them to write down as many chocolate items as they can think of in 30 seconds. The guest with the most items wins a chocolate prize. Be sure to have some of your guests read their answers—they can be quite entertaining.

- Party favors can be individually wrapped gourmet chocolates in a pretty gift bag.

Fall Tea Party

You can plan a fun tea party theme based on any of the four seasons. Welcome the cool, crisp days of autumn with a Fall Tea Party.

- Write the invitation on a real fall-colored leaf using a paint pen, or on a leaf shape cut from colored card stock. Or write the party details on small pumpkins and hand deliver them.

- Cover your serving table with a fall-colored tablecloth (burnt oranges, golden yellows, and autumn browns) or fall print fabric. Your centerpiece can be sunflowers or chrysanthemums in a hollowed-out pumpkin.

- Serve Apple Tea (page 13), Pumpkin Tea Bread (page 57), Apple Scones (page 25) with Brown Sugar & Cinnamon Butter (page 32), Pecan Tartlets (page 52), tea sandwiches cut into leaf shapes using a small cookie cutter, and petit fours cut into leaf shapes and iced with orange and red-orange icing. See page 60 for petit four instructions.

- For a fun activity, play the Fall Word Scramble game on page 83.

- Guest favors can be a fall-scented votive candle in a pretty organza draw-string bag.

Fall Word Scramble

Copy the following list. Give a pen and a copy of the list to each guest and ask them to unscramble as many of the words as they can in 3 minutes.

kipmunp	_____
spanec	_____
creacwors	_____
ahy leab	_____
spelap	_____
shevart omon	_____
sealve	_____
trofs	_____
nutamu	_____
kivgantshing	_____

answers: Pumpkin, pecans, scarecrow, hay bale, apples, harvest moon, leaves, frost, autumn, thanksgiving

Herb Garden Tea Party

An herb garden tea party is fun to have outside in the garden or on the porch or patio during the spring.

- Glue the invitation to the back of a packet of herb seeds and mail in an envelope. Ask your guests to wear pretty straw garden hats and spring colors.

- Use a colorful garden or herb print fabric to cover your table and make matching napkins if you sew.

- Your centerpiece can be a watering can filled with fresh herbs or several herb plants in terra cotta pots. Serve your food in terra cotta pots and saucers lined with garden-print fabric.

- Serve Herbal Tea Blend (page 18), Salmon & Dill Tea Sandwiches (page 42), Stuffed Cherry Tomatoes (page 48), Rosemary Mini Scones (page 31) with Herb Butter (page 34), Mint Nut Tea Bread (page 56) and Lavender Tea Cookies (page 73).

- For a fun activity give each guest a pen and piece of writing paper and see how many herbs they can write down in one minute. Or place a teaspoon of 8-10 dried herbs into tiny cups and ask your guests to identify them by sight and/or smell. The guest with the most correct answers wins a prize.

- The guests' favors can be tiny herb plants potted in mini-terra cotta pots, tied with ribbon.

"Always a Bridesmaid" Tea Party

Stage a fun tea party where your guests wear old bridesmaid's dresses or vintage formals from a second-hand clothing store.

- The invitation can be a fake, over-the-top wedding invitation, complete with plastic wedding bells attached with a satin bow. Mail in a tissue-lined box. Be sure to tell your guests to wear their favorite or most embarrassing bridesmaid's dress— with white gloves, of course!

- Cover your serving table with a white tablecloth and drape a tulle garland around the edge. Use silver candelabras for the centerpiece just like the cake table at a real wedding.

- Serve your treats from silver or crystal serving trays and tiered platters. All your food should be white, such as petit fours with white icing (page 60), Cream Scones (page 24) and Devonshire cream (page 35), Mini Cheesecakes (page 54), Chicken Salad Puffs (page 47) and Chive Cream Cheese Cucumber Tea Sandwiches (page 39).

- Serve one of the many varieties of white tea. If you don't have a store in your area that sells them, check out on-line sources. (See ordering information in the index.) White tea is a bit more expensive than other teas, but perfect for your special event.

- Have a fashion show where each guest models her gown on a runway. Take lots of pictures of your guests wearing their fabulous outfits. Or videotape the event and show the tape during the last half-hour of the party.

- Award each guest a "prize" for her costume (most outrageous, most colorful, most creative, most embarrassing, etc.).

- Party favors can be tiny nosegays of real or silk white roses for your guests to carry while modeling their dresses. Simply cut the stems of each flower to about 6" long and bundle about 5 or 6 blooms together (depending on their size). Wrap the stems with florist's tape and ribbon to hold them together.

Tea Time Brunch

A tea party doesn't have to be held in the afternoon. Why not treat your friends to a mid-morning brunch?

- Your theme can be "Rise and Shine!" The invitation might feature a cheerful sunrise scene or comical sun-shaped cut-out. You can enlarge the figure on page 88 using a copy machine and print it out onto yellow card stock. Cut out and embellish with an orange marker. Write your party details on the back in orange ink.

- The party colors will be sunny yellow and bright orange, so cover your serving table with a tablecloth or print fabric in these colors. The centerpiece can be a teapot filled with yellow daisies or orange chrysanthemums, depending on the season.

- Serve Apricot Orange Tea (page 13), Savory Sausage Scones (page 30), Mini Bacon Quiches (page 46), Peaches and Cream Mini-Muffins (page 59), Lemon Curd Tartlets (page 53) and Fruit and Cheese Mini Turnovers with Apricot filling (page 49).

- For a fun activity, play the Purse Scavenger Hunt Game on page 89.

- Send your guests off on a "sunny" note with sugar cookie favors in the shape of a sun cut-out, iced with yellow frosting and a happy face drawn with orange icing. Slip each one into a clear cellophane gift bag and tie with orange satin ribbon.

Enlarge the sun figure above on a copy machine and print out on yellow card stock. Cut out and embellish with an orange marker. Write your party details on the back in orange ink.

Purse Scavenger Hunt

Copy the following list. Give a pen and a copy of the form to each guest at your party. The guests are allowed 3 minutes to find as many of the following items as they can in their purses. The guest with the most items checked off the list wins the prize.

___Address book	___Hand cream
___Breath mints	___Lipstick
___Business card	___Mascara
___Calculator	___Mirror
___Candy	___Nail clippers
___Cell phone	___Pain reliever
___Chewing gum	___Pen
___Credit card	___Postage stamps
___Dental floss	___Rubber band
___Emery board	___Shopping list
___Eye glasses	___Tissue
___Eyelash curler	___Tooth brush
___Hair comb/brush	___Twenty dollar bill

Polka Dot Tea Party

Tea party themes based on shapes are great fun, and what could be more fun than colorful polka dots?

- Your invitation can be cut from polka dot paper. Be sure to ask your guests to wear their wildest polka dot outfits, including hats, shoes, gloves, accessories and purses.

- Cover the tea table with a polka dot tablecloth or polka dot print fabric (a mix of bright colors is best). The centerpiece can be a bundle of 6-8 colorful helium filled balloons tied with pretty ribbon (perhaps one for each guest). Use bright colored tea cups and teapots in a mix of solid colors like turquoise, royal blue, red, bright orange, sunny yellow and grass green.

- All of the food choices should be cut into circles including tea sandwiches (reinforce the dot theme by topping them with sliced, pimiento-stuffed olives), scones, savory appetizers like the mini-quiches on pages 45 and 46 and shrimp salad served on cucumber rounds, page 50. Serve sweets like mini-cheesecakes topped with cherry pie filling, page 54, and petit fours, page 60, cut into small circles and iced with bright colors. Present the food on round plates and platters in a mix of bright, solid colors.

- Take lots of pictures of your guests in their wild polka dot outfits and award a prize to each guest. You can use the balloons from your centerpiece for prizes. Label them: "Most Outrageous", Most Colorful", "Funniest", "Most Elegant", etc.

- For favors, purchase clear cellophane bags printed with polka dots and fill with colorful candy-coated chocolate pieces. Tie the bag closed with ribbon.

Teapot
Tea Party

Make those teapots talk! Invite your fellow tea party lovers to a party that's all about their favorite teapots.

- Your invitation must be in the shape of a teapot. Use the one on page 77 if you like. Ask each guest to bring her favorite teapot to the party: either a family heirloom, a gift from a special friend, a unique second-hand find or one she just fell in love with and had to own. You might also ask your guests to come dressed for a "traditional" tea party: pretty dresses, white gloves and hats if they like.

- Cover your tea table with a teapot-print tablecloth or fabric. Your centerpiece can be an arrangement of all the teapots your guests bring. Raise them at different heights using fabric covered boxes to create a more interesting display.

- Use a teapot-shaped cookie cutter to cut out tea sandwiches, scones and petit fours. Serve several different flavors of tea, each in a different teapot, so you can show off your own teapot collection.

- Let the teapots reveal their stories. Have each guest tell why the teapot she brought is her favorite.

- For a fun activity ask your guests to write down their answers to the following question: If you were a tea party treat (petit four, tea sandwich, cake, scone, flavored spread, savory appetizer, cookie, etc.) what would you be and why? Collect the answers and read them aloud to see if the other guests can guess who wrote each one.

- Guest favors can be large sugar cookies cut out in the shape of teapots and iced with colorful icing and pretty icing flowers. You can also write each guest's name on a cookie using icing. Place in a clear cellophane bag and tie closed with satin ribbon.

Fortune Telling Tea Party

Surprise your friends with a mysterious, intriguing fortune-telling tea party.

- Your invitation should be cut from deep purple card stock. Add metallic gold stickers in the shapes of moons and stars. Write the information inside using a metallic gold paint pen. Ask your guests to wear deep purple and any gypsy-like attire they choose (scarves, shawls, heavy gold jewelry, etc.)

- Cover your table with a purple tablecloth or a print that has gold celestial symbols (moons and stars). Use a gold garden gazing ball for your centerpiece.

- Most of the food should be purple, such as blueberry muffins and mini cheesecakes topped with blueberry pie filling, page 54. Blueberry scones; flavored cream cheese tea sandwiches, page 39, and petit fours, page 60, (coated with yellow icing) can be cut into the shapes of moons and stars using cookie cutters.

- For a fun activity, try reading tea leaves. You can hire a professional reader of tea leaves or try it yourself using the instructions on page 96. For more information about reading tea leaves, check your local library or book store.

- Favors can be gold fold-wrapped chocolates inside purple velvet drawstring bags.

Reading the Tea Leaves

- Use smooth, shallow tea cups that have white interiors. Use loose tea with large leaves, and brew the tea in each cup instead of a teapot.

- Place about a teaspoon of tea in each cup and fill with boiling water. As the tea steeps the leaves will settle to the bottom of the cup.

- Make a wish or think of a question while drinking the tea.

- Leave about a teaspoon of tea in the bottom of the cup. Using the left hand, swirl the tea three times in a clockwise motion to spread the leaves around the sides of the cup, then turn it upside down onto the saucer to drain.

- Turn the cup right side up and look for a picture. The first one you see is the answer to the question you thought of while drinking the tea.

- The placement of the pictures in the cup is important. Leaves on the bottom of the cup foretell the distant future, on the sides tell the not too distant future, and on the rim area tell the present. The pictures or symbols that you see very clearly are more significant than those that are unclear.

Below are a few interpretations of the tea leaf pictures:

Anchor - success in business
Arch - a journey
Angel - good news
Arrow - bad news
Birds - good news or travel by air
Bouquet - luckiest symbol, fulfillment of desires
Butterfly - anticipated pleasure
Cat - treachery if in the bottom of the cup
Crescent Moon - changes
Circle - wedding - trust and love
Dog - good and faithful friends
Fish - very good fortune
Fork - a change in directions
Fruits - if in season, contentment
Heart - love
Horseshoe - good luck, prosperity
Kite - long journey
Knife - arguments
Ladder - advancement
Lines - advancement, long life
Mouth - listen carefully
Rainbow - good luck to come
Ring - marriage
Scissors - separation
Square - comfort
Sun - warmth and happiness
Tree - wishes will come true
Triangle - unforeseen legacy

Afternoon Tea Party Club

If you have several friends who enjoy having afternoon tea on a regular basis, why not form an "Afternoon Tea Party Club"?

Plan to stage the event once a month, with each member of the group taking a turn hosting it at her home. A tea party club is especially fun because the guests take more of an interest in researching tea-time history, etiquette and recipes.

Your monthly teas can be centered around the activity of "taking tea", or held in conjunction with another activity, such as a book club. Afternoon tea parties are even more appropriate if your club reviews books of one particular genre, such as historical romance.

Having a theme for your tea party makes the planning easier, and enables the guests to be more interactive, especially when asked to wear a costume, a hat, a color or print pattern.

Your theme can be based on a color ("pretty in pink" or "red hot mama's"), a shape (stars, stripes or polka dots), a flower (roses, sunflowers or lavender), a flavor (chocolate, strawberries or orange), a place (seaside, garden or French bistro), a historical period (Southern Plantation or Roaring Twenties), a holiday or a season (winter wonderland or summer picnic).

To plan a theme tea party, make a list of every item, food, color, costume, activity or fact that fits into your theme. You might need to do some research for historical periods or foreign countries, but it will make your theme more authentic. The things you select from your list will be your guide for choosing the colors, decorations, food and activities for your party.

And don't forget to start with a unique invitation, such as a tiny straw hat with the party details attached and mailed in a small box for a garden theme; or the details written on a small pumpkin and hand-delivered for a fall theme.

Each event is not only fun, but challenging, as the hostess puts her creative talents to work in order to surprise and delight the other club members.

Start an afternoon tea party club with a group of tea-loving friends so you can enjoy fun-filled tea parties on a regular basis.

In no time at all, your teapots will have lot of things to talk about!

Teatime tip: For an unusual treat, consider using "blooming" (display) teas at your tea party. These are made by hand-sewing tea leaves around a center flower. They are a delight for the eyes and the taste buds, as the blooms unfurl when added to water. See ordering information in the index.

Make Memories with Tea

Take a brief time out to relax and enjoy the company of friends while sharing afternoon tea and delectable treats on your prettiest china.

Use the teatime tips, tasty recipes and fun party ideas in this book to host lots of beautiful tea parties to lavish on yourself and others.

Get out those teapots and create fond memories with lively conversation and laughter and fun.

If your teapots could talk, what stories would they tell?

Enjoy!

Recipe Index

Ordering Sources for Tea, Herbs and Tea Accessories:

Adagio Teas
www.adagio.com
- blooming (display) teas
- white teas, wide range of flavored teas
- many tea blends in teabags
- teapots, glass teapots and cups for display teas
- tea balls and infusers, paper tea filters

Devotea
www.devotea.com
- tea cozies
- children's tea sets
- teatime stationery, napkins
- teapot picture frames
- teapots, teapot spoons

San Francisco Herb Company
www.sfherb.com
- dried herbs, culinary lavender and rose petals
- white tea, flavored teas
- sealable, empty tea bags
- tea balls and infusers
- cellophane bags

The Tea Table
www.theteatable.com
- sugar tongs, decorated sugar cubes
- flowering teas, flavored teas
- unique shaped doilies
- cookie cutters
- teapot spoons, infusers, teapots

About the Author

Gloria Hander Lyons has channeled 30 years of training and hands-on experience in the areas of art, interior decorating, crafting and event planning into writing creative how-to books.

Her books cover a wide range of topics including decorating your home, cooking, planning weddings and tea parties, crafting and self publishing.

She has designed original needlework and craft projects featured in magazines, including *Better Homes and Gardens, McCall's, Country Handcrafts* and *Crafts.*

Gloria also teaches interior decorating, self publishing and wedding planning classes at her local community college and offers private classes and workshops.

Much to her family's delight, her kitchen is in non-stop test mode, creating recipes for new cookbooks.

Check out her monthly newsletter for free craft ideas, decorating and event planning tips and taste-tempting recipes at **www.BlueSagePress.com**.

Other Books by Gloria Hander Lyons

- *Easy Microwave Desserts in a Mug*
- *Easy Microwave Desserts in a Mug for Kids*
- *Teapots and Teddy Bears: Fun Children's Tea Parties*
- *No Rules—Just Fun Decorating*
- *Just Fun Decorating for Tweens & Teens*
- *Decorating Basics: For Men Only!*
- *The Super Bride's Guide for Dodging Wedding Pitfalls*
- *A Taste of Lavender: Delectable Treats with an Exotic Floral Flavor*
- *Lavender Sensations: Fragrant Herbs for Home & Bath*
- *Designs That Sell: How To Make Your Home Show Better & Sell Faster*
- *Self-Publishing On a Budget: A Do-It-All-Yourself Guide*
- *The Secret Ingredient: Tasty Recipes with an Unusual Twist*
- *Hand Over the Chocolate and No One Gets Hurt! The Chocolate-Lover's Cookbook*

For a complete list of books visit our website:
www.BlueSagePress.com

Ordering Information

To order additional copies of this book, send check or money order payable to:

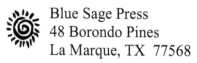 Blue Sage Press
48 Borondo Pines
La Marque, TX 77568

Cost is $8.95 for this edition (U.S. Currency)

Shipping & Handling Charges: $3.50 for the first book and $1.50 for each additional book shipped to the same address in the U.S.A.

Texas residents add 8.25% sales tax to total order amount.

To pay by credit card or get a complete list of books, visit our website: www.BlueSagePress.com